Python Made Easy 1

The Ultimate Step by Step Guide for Beginners

Subscribe to our mailing list at

www.AshPublishing.net

Hacking Series Books
By Alexander Sycamore

Hacking Made Easy 1

Hacking Made Easy 2

Python Made Easy 1

Table of Contents

Introduction

Thank you for purchasing the book *Python Made Easy 1*.

This book contains proven steps and strategies on how to become a true expert on the uses of Python and how it can help you in different aspects of your life when it comes to computer programming.

Here is an inescapable fact: you can use Python for both computer programing and hacking!

Programming is not an easy task, you need to make sure that you have plenty of patience and logical thinking for what you want to do with your code. Not only that but you need to be diligent so you do not mess up and have to rewrite your entire code.

Let's get into the learning process right away!

Chapter One:
What is Python?

Python is a computer programming language that can be used across all platforms and machines that a code writer will use. Python has different functions that canhelp make coding easier while making the codes look better and easier to read.

While we think of a rather large, heavy bodied constrictor snake when we hear Python, there is actually no relevance. Back in 1990, when the program was created by Guido von Rossum, it was named after the British comedy, *Monty Python's Flying Circus.*

Python is a coding program that is easily available and helps to simplify finding a solution for a computer problem. This program runs much like if you had taken the time to sit and write out your solution to the problem on paper, except that it is done with a computer.

The great thing about Python is that it can be run on any computer and you will not need to change the program once it has been written.

When the program was first developed in the nineties, a team of volunteers had been running the program. This program and even support can be reached by going to the website for the Python Software Foundation at https://www.Python.org. During September of 2006, Python 2.5 was released. This is the most recent version of Python available.

When you look at the different versions of Python, you will see there was a Java version of Python called Jython. Jython was to be used when the coder was using a Java coding program.

Iron Python uses the C# version that works with .Net and Mono platforms. Anyone who uses C# has the same flexibility and power of Python. It is much like they are using Python, without using it.

But, as any programmer knows, each program is going to be different. While Python is written in one language, it will work off that language as its primary while working and interacting with other languages. This is just one of the many modules built into Python while it was being developed.

The PyPy project was founded in 2003 to help Python programmers be able to change how Python worked with the interpreter that helps it to communicate with other programming languages. The project was an open sourced project, therefore, allowing it to be developed by a community of developers for free distribution and modification should the need for modification arise. This project was also founded by the Python Foundation and the European Union. This was funded as part of the FP6 program under STReP (Specified Targeted Research Program).

Python can be used across any modern operating system and can be used to process things such as:

Scientific data

Images

Text

Numbers

Or anything else that you can save on your computer.

Many people do not realize that websites we use every day were coded using Python. Websites such as YouTube and Google were coded using Python. NASA and the New York Stock Exchange were coded using Python as well. However, those are just a few websites that Python has made possible for us to access. There are businesses, government, and non-profit organization websites that run off of Python coding as well.

Since Python is an interpreted language, it need not be converted for a program to run off of it. This differs from the languages of the past that had to be converted due to them being a scripting language. The scripting languages were made to imitate how it operated for the banal and trivial tasks that needed to be done. However, Python and several other programs like it were made so they were different have been forced to change in that nomenclature.

The syntax and commands used by Pythondiffer from any other interpreted language. For example, Perl is being displaced by PHP as the lingua franca of a down and dirty web development program. But, unlike Perl or even PHP, Python is easier to follow and easier to read.

The squirrely code shared by Perl and PHP is one of the major flaws for these two programs. The syntax of PHP and Perl causes it to be harder to write a code that exceeds fifty to one hundred lines. However, Python, makes it easier to extend and maintain the code liens because of how easily readable it is. This is one of the hard wired modules in the very fabric of Python's language.

For a more general web-oriented programming language PHP is one of the better ones out there. PHP stands for 'Hypertext Processor,' which means that it is meant to output a web readable information instead of system level tasks. You can use Python to develop a web serve that will understand PHP language. Sadly, it cannot be reversed to where PHP will understand Python though.

Python is an object oriented program and PHP is not. Because of this, the maintainability, scalability, and even the readability can mess with how the program is written.

When you look at the programming languages out there, you will notice they can be used for different fields of careers such as:

Artificial Intelligence Development: this is dedicated to making AIs or cognitive systems, that can interact with human behavior and learn what they are programmed to learn. Programs made here include character interactions on computer games, parts of programs that make decisions, and chat boxes that can reply back to the sender.

Application and Program Development: these involve programs you work with daily. An internet browser program you use to view your favorite web pages, or an application that allows you to read e-books such as this on your Kindle, are examples of programs made this way.

Database Development: self-explanatory. You make and maintain mini-databases, which hold large quantities of digital information for people to look up and use. These are important for websites to have so they can compile information.

Game Development: self-explanatory as well. Computer games and other entertainment software can be written by language programs such as Java. The flash games you find online are using the exact same script.

Computer Drivers or other hardware interface development: programs made with this focus on mind support hardware functionality.

Internet and web page development: the lifeblood of the internet. Without developers, there would be no web pages, and without web pages, there would be no internet.

Script development: the knowledge on how to make scripts that will benefit any company's productivity.

As you can see, Python can be very helpful in different aspects of our everyday life. We use things coded by Python every day and do not even realize it. Python literally helps to keep our lives running because without it, we would not have the easily readable code that makes up the different programs we use to do things such as, online banking, entertainment, or even having a computer.

Chapter Two:
Why Should You Learn Python?

The awesome thing about Python is that it is an interpreted and interactive programming language. Interpreted simply means it need not be compiled before it is executed, but it still requires an interpreter for the script to be modified. Python is also an object oriented coding language that makes it possible to interact or even execute multiple programs at once.

The best thing about Python is that it is the easiest and most user friendly programming language around. Rather than being created to look ugly, it was created to look pretty, it is explicit rather than vague, and it is easy to read. However, do not be mistaken that Python is going to be easy to work with. It is still a complex programming language. But, if you put in the work and practice using it as well as being diligent with the material you are working with, it will become simple for you to use.

When you are first learning how to code, you may want to consider getting a program that is free and simple for you to use as you are learning. The program will thrive on being simple, and you can even make a few short cut commands.

Because Python is easy to use, it is easy to learn how to use. Python's overall structure is easy for those who are new to programming to master and is fairly clear on how it is run. Since Python runs off a high level language, the strings are copied together in a clear and easy syntax that has but a few commands.

As you are learning how to master Python, you will notice that you are going to be able to code the more complicated scripts that would usually take minutes to hours for someone to program. The scripting languages used by Python, make programming variants fast and easy. This way, you can create scripts that will simplify everyday work, therefore,Python is the program of choice.

Being easy to read is not important, but it is however a great asset when looking for a scripting language. For example, if you are running Perl, the code will probably end up looking a lot like hieroglyphics. But, Python will descramble the code and make it to where you are more likely to remember what the source code you wrote does.

Python has a large set of modules that will help you with anything that you need for writing source code. The downside is that you will need to elaborate in order to fully be able to discover the ins and outs of the more complex modules.

The biggest thing that Python users enjoy about this program is that it can be used across multiple platforms. This makes it very useful because sometimes several operating systems are used when working with source codes. Python can also run on any machine you need it to run on. Therefore, you can run whatever scripts you create almost anywhere you are.

Python can also cross platforms such as GUIs or Qt. this can cause any GUIs you have created not having to be readjusted for the source code every time you need to switch to a new machine.

Chapter Three:
Installing Python

To use Python, you will need to download it if you have not already. You are going to want to get the latest version of Python, which is 2.7, from the official Python website. Within this chapter, I will teach you how to download Python for different operating systems.

Windows

To download the latest version for Python 2, go to:
https://www.Python.org/downloads/release/Python-2712/

Select the MSI package for the Windows download. To install it manually, you are just going to double-click on the downloaded file. The MSI package format allows any Windows administrators to automate the installation with their standard tools.

Note there 2 kinds of Python downloads available, namely Python 2 and Python 3. Python 2 is the legacy version of the programming language whereas Python 3 is the present and future. However, due to potentially compatibility issues that may arise from Python 3, we will use Python 2 throughout this book.

Python 2.7.12

Release Date: 2016-06-25

Python 2.7.12 is a bugfix release in the Python 2.7.x series.

Full Changelog

Files

After downloading, double click on the file to install and complete the process.

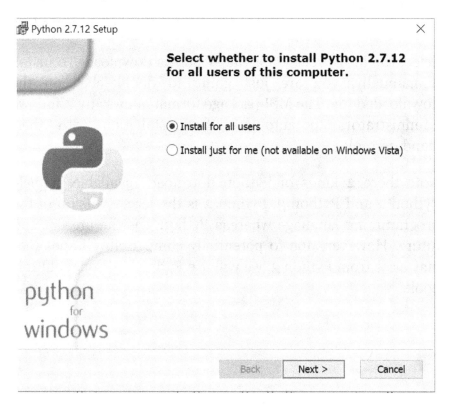

By design, Python installs a directory with the version number embedded into it. For example, Python version 2.7 will install as C:\Python27\. You are able to download any of the older or newer versions of Python and not have to ever worry about a version conflict. Only one interpreter will be the defaulted application for the Python file types. It will not automatically modify the environment variable of path, or location on the computer file or webpage so you can always have control which copy of Python runs.

If typing the full path name for the Python every time feels tedious, do not worry; you can add the directories for your default Python version to the PATH. Therefore, if your Python installation is in C:\Python27\, then you can add this to your PATH:

C:\Python27\;C:\Python27\Scripts\

You can do this easily by running the following in PowerShell:

[Environment]::SetEnvironmentVariable("Path", "$env:Path;C:\Python27\;C:\Python27\Scripts\", "User")

A second directory script will receive the command files when certain packages are installed, so this addition helps a lot. You will not need to install or configure anything else to use Python. But, it is strongly recommended that you install the tools and libraries before you build Python applications to be used in the real world. In particular, you should always install the Setuptools software, as it makes it much easier for you to use other third party Python libraries.

Mac OS X

When using Mac, you will not need to install or even configure anything to use Python. However, you should install the tools and libraries much like you would have if you were using Windows.

The download link can also be found here: https://www.Python.org/downloads/release/Python-2712/

The version of Python that ships with OS X is good for learning how to use Python, however it is not good for development. That is due to the version being out of date with the official and most current release out for Python.

Before you install the up to date version, you are going to need to install GCC. GCC is going to be obtained by downloading Xcode, the smaller Command Line Tools. This will require you to have an Apple account. If you do not want GCC, then you can download the smaller OSX-GCC Installer package.

Note: If you already have Xcode, you need not install OSX-GCC Installer. Having both programs will cause a conflict while trying to run on your computer. Also, if you do a fresh install of your Xcode, you need to add the command line tools by running Xcode-select—install on the terminal.

OS X comes with a large amount of UNIX utilities. If you are familiar with the Linux system, you will notice there is one key component missing. A decent package manager. This can be fixed by installing Homebrew. Open either your favorite OSX terminal emulator or Python Terminal so you can run this command:

$ /usr/bin/ruby -e "$(curl –fsSL https://raw.githubusercontent.com/Homebrew/install/master/install)"

The script then will explain what changes it will need to make and then prompt you before the actual instillation begins.

After the installation is done, you will now insert your new Homebrew directory at the top of the PATH environment variable. This can be done using this command: **export PATH=/usr/local/bin:/usr/local/sbin:$PATH**.

At this point you can now install Python 2.7 with the $ brew install Python command and then you will have everything installed and ready for use in just a few minutes.

Linux

Version 2.7 is one of the many of the latest versions available on the Linux system. You can however check to see what Python version you have using the $ Python –version command.

The older versions of RHEL and CentOS will come with Python 2.4 instead. However, there are extra packages for enterprise Linux from the Python website that can be downloaded.

Setuptools + Pip:

Setuptools extends the packaging and even the installation facilities provided by the distuils in the standard library and is one of the most important third-party tools you will need to use Python. Once you have added in Setuptools, you can download and install any compliant Python software with a single command. This also enables you to add this network installation capability to your own Python software with little work.

You can also find thelatest version of Setuptools for Windows by running the Python script: ex setup.py. From here you will then have a new command available to use: easy install.

However, since many will criticize the use of this and that it is bad to use it, use the command pip instead. Using Pip will allow you to uninstall any packages and is actively maintained unlike when you use easy install.

Now that you have Pip installed, with the following Python script: gig-pip.py. Using this method will help with installation when using a Mac OS X computer. Pip will automatically install in Linux centric Python programs 2.7.9 and beyond and 3.4 and beyond. To make sure that Pip is installed, run the command $ command -v pip.

Virtual Environments:

The virtual environment is a tool that will help you to keep the dependencies required by different projects in separate places. This is done by creating virtual Python environments for them. In doing this, you will not have to worry about problems like "project X depends on version 1.x but, project y needs 4.x", and you can keep your global site packages directory clean.

Chapter Four:
Using Python

You now have Python installed on your computer and you are ready to use it. However, there are different ways that Python can be used and we will go over them in this chapter.

Python as we have said, is an easy to use programming language and is relatively simple to learn as you are attempting to learn how to write your own source code for whatever it is you are wanting to use Python for.

You should follow every step as you are going through trying to learn how to use Python for the many different uses that it allows you to use it with. If you do not, you are more than likely going to end up doing something that you do not want to do when it comes to writing out source code. You need to be patient and diligent with your work as you are going through this.

If you do not have the time to sit and put in the time to practice using Python, you will end up finding out that it will take you longer to use the program than if you took the time and practiced on it.

Practice as much as you can while you are using Python so you know how to use every aspect of Python and that you are not missing out on any of the many things that Python offers for you to use.

Using the Python Interpreter as a Calculator

Step one: Open your command prompt and type the word Python into the prompt and press enter. By doing this, the interpreter will then open and you will be taken to the command prompt.

```
C:\Windows\System32\cmd.exe - python                          —    □    ×
Microsoft Windows [version 10.0.10586]
(c) 2015 Microsoft Corporation. Tous droits réservés.

C:\WINDOWS\system32>python
Python 2.7.10 (default, May 23 2015, 09:44:00) [MSC v.1500 64 bit (AMD64)] on wi
n32
Type "help", "copyright", "credits" or "license" for more information.
>>>
```

If you did not integrate Python into your command prompt, you will need to go directly into the Python directory to get the interpreter running.

Step Two: now with the interpreter open, you can use Python to do basic arithmetic.

Please note: if you see # then it means that your code did not go through the interpreter. You can either try and put it through again, or rewrite your code to make sure that it will go through.

Step Three: by using Python as a calculator, you can signify powers by using the ** operator. While using this function, Pythoncan quickly calculate any large numbers.

Step Four: you can now assign different variables while in Python to have Python do basic algebra. Doing this will then help you to introduce and assign different variables later in your programming. The variables are assigned by using the = sign.

Step Five: once your calculations are done, you will now need to close your interpreter. To do this, press Ctrl+Z and then press enter. Alternatively, you can type quit() into the command prompt and press enter as well.

Creating Your First Program:

Step One: the first step is to create a test program that will allow you to use the basics of creating and saving any programs you create with the interpreter. This is also another way for you to test and make sure that your interpreter is working correctly.

Step Two: "Print" is a basic function Python uses. Print will display information in the terminal for any programming you are doing.

Note: "print" is one of the biggest changes introduced inPython 3.

While using Python 2, you had to type the word "print" forwhat you wanted to be displayed on your screen. However, with Python 3, "print" is a function you only need to type "print()" with whatever you want displayed typed inside the parentheses.

Step Three: the most common way you can test the program is to add in display text. The text "Hello World!" should be placed within the "print()" statement that must include the quotation marks.

But, unlike other programming languages, you will not need to designate when a line ends with a;. Also, you will not need to use {} to denote where blocks are. Instead, you will indent to signify what is included in a block.

Step Four: once you are finished, you will need to save your file. To do this, you will click on the file menu and then click save as just like you were trying to save a Word document. In the drop down menu, right beneath the name box you will choose what your Python file type is.

Should you be using regular Notepad, you will select all files and add .pv to the end of your file name.

Note: make sure that you save the file somewhere you can easily find again later!

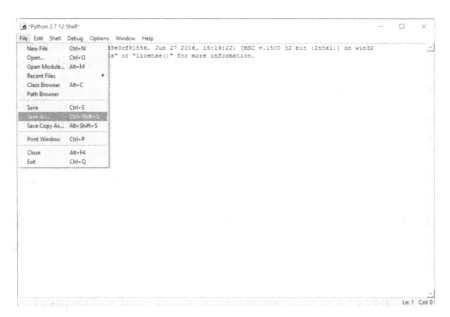

Step Five: at this point in time, you are going to need to reopen your command prompt and navigate back to the location in which you saved your file. As soon as you are where you need to be, you will then run the file by typing in the name of the file. Or Python3 file name.py to run your program.

Step Six: one of the great things about using Python is that you can test out any new programs instantly. Close the command prompt and the editor before you reopen them and test to see if any changes need to be made. Questions must be made immediately.

Building Advanced Program:

Step one: to control what a program does based on specific conditions is called a flow control statement. Statements like this are the heart of what Python programming does and then will allow you to create a program that will do different things depending on what you input into it and your conditions. The while statement is good to start with.

```
# Example of control flow with the while loop

i =                     # Statements before the while loop
while i < 5 :           # While loop condition

    print "i still < 5"   # Body of the while loop

    i = i +1

print "now i > 5 "        # Statements after the while loop

<statements before while loop>
while <condition>:
<body of while loop>
<statements after the while loop>
```

25

Step Two: any function can be defined and then later called on while in a program. You will find this to be useful when using multiple functions within the confines of a larger program.

Step Three: the flow control statements allow you to set specific conditions to change how a program runs. This comes in handy when dealing with user input later on.

Step Four: mathematical symbols such as the greater than and less than symbols are used in Python except they are used a little differently.

Step Five: make sure that you never stop learning. Go to the Python website and read the documents they provide for their users. Research any questions that you have on Python and always keep your Python versions updated and tested to make sure that you are running everything as it should be.

Chapter Five:
Building a Website with Python

Python can be used for a wide variety of things. You can use it for hacking and even video game creations. All these things we will talk about in a later chapter. But, in this chapter, we will talk about how you can use Python to build a website.

Do not worry if the programming you write does not come out how you are wanting it to come out the first time. It is important to remember that you are able to use Python in such a way that will allow you to make temporary programs that will not affect your finished project.

When you look at websites such as Google and YouTube, you may not know it, but they are built using Python as we have mentioned earlier. However, you will be using the Flask framework to build your own website from scratch. Flask is easy to learn and even simple to get started with.

First, you will need to insert something that looks like the coding below into an empty text.

Note: Make sure that you always save your work with the title and then .py on the end.

```
from flask import Flask

app = Flask(__name__)

@app.route('/')
def home():
return "Hey there!"

if __name__ == '__main__':
```

app.run(debug=True)

```
*Untitled*                                               —   □   ×
File  Edit  Format  Run  Options  Window  Help
from flask import Flask

app = Flask(__name__)

@app.route('/')
def home():
    return "Hey there!"

if __name__ == '__main__':
    app.run(debug=True)




                                                      Ln: 11  Col: 0
```

Please take notice that flask is imported from the library from the first line of coding. In case you have no library installed, you will then receive an error code that will not allow you to proceed.

If you need to install flask, just type pip install flask into the command line of Python. Once you have made sure that flask is indeed installed properly, run your test script.

As soon as your script is running properly, the website will run on your local machine and can be viewed by typing in localhost:5000 in the browser you use.

At this point in time your website will just be plain text. You should make sure that it works before you go adding in the different designs and such that will make it look like a website.

The first thing you need to think about is who will be using your website? This will affect what data you put into the coding and what you make your website look like.

Being a developer, you will need to write the code in Python to handle the requests from the users to be visiting your website and the CGI. This is a standard environment that Python and many other web development programming languages use for them to create web pages.

Since this is such a repetitive task, you can put all your code together and create a bunch of Python files. These files are known as flask. Flask is the framework loaded within Python to automatically execute the routine code. This will also allow you to focus on specific parts of your website you need to fix at a later date.

So, if you type pip install flask in your command line, you are installing the flask framework from its repositories. However, when you import flask, you are making the framework available for your current script.

So, your coding should look a little something like this:

1. from flask import Flask

2. app = Flask(__name__)

3. @app.route('/')

4. def home():

5. return "Hey there!"

6. if __name__ == '__main__':

7. app.run(debug=True)

```
flask_import.py - C:/Users/Diallo-Pc/Desktop/flask_import.py (2.7.12)          —    □    ×

File  Edit  Format  Run  Options  Window  Help
from flask import Flask

app = Flask(__name__)

@app.route('/')
def home():
    return "Hey there!"

if __name__ == '__main__':
    app.run(debug=True)
```
Ln: 10 Col: 23

With one line; all code that is needed in order to build a web app using flask is located here. Simply put, flask if your prototype that will be used to create instances of web application.

Once flask is imported, you will then create an instance of flask class that will be able to help you with your web app. Line three does the same this with the name (_name_). This is a special variable that gets valued as the string "_main_" when you are actually executing the script.

It is lines five through seven that are going to be your defining functions that return the string. These functions are mapped to the home '/' URL. Therefore, the user will be able to navigate to localhost:5000 and then the home function will be returned to its original output on the webpage. If the input route method was something different, for example, '/about/' then the user would be directed to localhose: 5000/about/.

Lines nine and ted have the "_main_" script. If the script is imported into a different script, then the script will keep its original name. but, in our case, we are using _name_ which will be equal to "_main_". Should the conditional statement be satisfied, then the app.run() will be executed. This allows the programmer to have control over how the script behaves.

You will also notice that you have set the debug parameter to true. This will put the possible python errors on the web page therefore helping to trace any errors in the script. While you are in the production environment, you will want to set it to false.

If you want to make something more visually appealingyou will want to incorporate some HTML files. This will return the HTML pages instead of just plain strings of text.

This is where you will learn how to return HTML pages with the render_template method.

You should see that there is not any plain text and that the text you have can have various formats. This is made by returning the HTML template rather than the plain text from python.

To do this, you will want to create an empty file with the name of something similar to home.html and put the following code into it.

```
<!DOCTYPE html>

<html>

<body>

<h1>My Personal Website</h1>
```

```
<p>Hi, this is my personal website.</p>

</body>

</html>
```

HTML is the language that web pages use. You will need to make sure that you remember these three important things when it comes to creating HTML pages.

- Any visible part of the HTML will be between <body> and </body>. The areas outside of this are used in reference to Javascript files, CSS or any similar features.

- The HTML document needs to start with a declaration that will specify the document type: <!DOCTYPEhtml>

- HTML documents will always begin with <html> and end with </html/>

In the flask framework, there should be a folder that was written so that it specifically looks for HTML template files. This folder should be called templates.

Any python scripting will stay outside of the templates folder as it is not HTML.

The code to be able to read the HTML templates will look similar to this. Note: this is the updated code from our flask code earlier.

```
from flask import Flask, render_template

app = Flask(__name__)

@app.route('/')
```

```
def home():
    return render_template('home.html')
if __name__ == '__main__':
    app.run(debug=True)
```

You will notice that the code was updated by using the imported render_template method within the flak framework. It is from here that the HTML files are on the flask framework. This will generate a jinja 2 template then return the template to the browser whenever the users visits your URL.

If you are wanting to create an "about" page, you will need to create another HTML file in the template folder. The coding for this is going to look a little something like this:

```
<!DOCTYPE html>

<html>

<body>

<h1>About me</h1>

<p>This is a portfolio site about anything that can be put in a portfolio.</p>

</body>

</html>
```

It is from here that you will be able to render the HTML you created with python by adding a second function to the template. The new code for this looks like this:

```
from flask import Flask, render template

app = Flask(__name__)
```

```python
@app.route('/')
def home():
    return render_template('home.html')

@app.route('/about/')
def about():
    return render_template('about.html')

if __name__ == '__main__':
    app.run(debug=True)
```

Once you have put the last string of code in, you will then need to run the scrip localhost:5000/about and this will open a new page. At a later date, this template can have CSS styling applied to it in order to make it look like you want it to look.

The updated coding for about.html is going to look something similar to this:

```html
<!DOCTYPE html>

<html>

<body>

<div class="about">

<h1>About me</h1>

<p>This is a portfolio site about anything that can be put in a portfolio.</p>

</div>

</body>

</html>
```

You'll have to do this for your home.html as well.

```
<!DOCTYPE html>

<html>

<body>

<div class="home">

<h1>About me</h1>

<p>This website was built with Python via the Flask framework.</p>

</div>

</body>

</html>
```

When you run your python script now, you will now have two URLs open. It is at this point in time that you should have two HTML pages as well as the python script that has resulted in your HTML pages being two different URLs. These two URLs are your home page as well as your about page.

If you are wanting to create an area in each page, you will then need to add in the HTML code that will cause a header to generate for each file. However, before you do this, the smart thing would be to create a parent HTML template that your later templates will then inherit the code from. This is done by simply linking the parent template to each HTML page so that they can inherit the code.

The first step is to create a new page that you wll call layout.html and the coding will look like this:

```html
<!DOCTYPE html>

<html>

<body>

<header>

<div class="container">

<h1 class="logo">Ardit's web app</h1>

<strong><nav>

<ul class="menu">

<li><a href="{{ url_for('home') }}">Home</a></li>

<li><a href="{{ url_for('about') }}">About</a></li>

</ul>

</nav></strong>

</div>

</header>

</body>

</html>
```

Python will then modify the home and about.html pages as well as your layout.html files. At this point, you will then need to link the about.html, home.html all to the layout.html. this is going to take a few lines of coding and you are going to start with the layout.html.

```html
<!DOCTYPE html>
<html>
<body>
<header>
<div class="container">
<h1 class="logo">Ardit's web app</h1>
<strong><nav>
<ul class="menu">
<li><a href="{{ url_for('home') }}">Home</a></li>
<li><a href="{{ url_for('about') }}">About</a></li>
</ul>
</nav></strong>
</div>
</header>
<div class="container">
{% block content %}
{% endblock %}
</div>
</body>
</html>
```

You will notice that a new div section was added to your layout.html. the two lines within the curly brackets will then be replaced on demand in either the home.html or the about.html code, depending on which URL the user is using at the time. But, in order for these to work, you will then need to edit both your about and home pages so that they will connect to your layout page.

Your home.html code will look like this:

```
{% extends "layout.html" %}

{% block content %}

<div class="home">

<h1>A Python product</h1>

<p>This website was built with Python via the Flask framework.</p>

</div>

{% endblock %}
```

And this is what your about.html will look like:

```
{% extends "layout.html" %}

{% block content %}

<div class="about">

<h1>About me</h1>

<p>This is a portfolio site about anything that can be put in a portfolio.</p>
```

```
</div>

{% endblock %}
```

Congratulations!

You now have a functional website! However, you are still missing some of your website. These were just the basics of how to make a website by using Python coding. You can still add more to your website like CSS styling and finally the steps that you will need to make your website public in the lessons that can be found on www.pythonhow.com

Chapter Six:
Other Uses for Python

When you look at all the things you can do with Python, you will learn that you can actually create video games with the Python source coding and use Python for hacking into computer systems.

Note: it is important to not hack into any system without the expressed written permission from the system administrator.

Game Creation

When creating a game using Python, you will use PyGame. This software adds the functionality on top of the SDL library. It allows you to create fully featured games and multimedia programs by using the Python language.

Pygame allows the game to be highly portable and run off of nearly every platform and operating

There are numerous examples and documentation of games created by using PyGame that have succeeded. You will also find it is easy to write games and graphic intensive programs by using PyGame.

If you are wanting to make a high level game that is in 3-D, you will use PySoy. This works with the engine used on Python 3. Python 3 tightly binds the rendering physics, networking, and even the animation.

Python-Ogre is the complete Python wrapper for the OGRE 3D engine that includes fifteen other graphics and gaming related libraries used for GUI, special effects, sound, physics, and many more.

There are several other libraries you can look at or will need to make a game. If you are wanting to look into these libraries, you can go to:
www.wiki.Python.org/moin/PythonGames

You will also see there is something call PyWeek, which is a bi-annual challenge that will produce several great games. It is a challenge where you can show off your programming skills and create a game that will go up against other games in proving that you are the best.

Hacking

We have all see hacking in the movies and on tv shows and how it looks like it is so exciting and there are meaningless ones and zeros just flying across the screen. Watching it makes it seem like hacking is magical.

However, it is not magical. It is based on computers and when it comes to computers, everything that is done has logical principles behind it so that it can be learned and understood. Even if you do not understand why a computer does what it does, there is also going to be a reason why it did that.

It is not hard to learn why it does what it does why a computer does what it does. All it takes is a little time and patience in learning.

When you are hacking, you are attempting to get into someone's operating system. This is done by hacking into the encrypted coding that is surrounding the computer. Once you have done this, you are then able to look at the files that are on the system that you have hacked into.

By using Python, you are able to change the code so that you are able to get into the operating system. The bad thing about this is that if you are changing things within an operating system, the system administrator will be able to notice that you have changed things and then will know that they have been hacked.

If you are going to hack someone, as we have mentioned at the beginning of this chapter, you are going to need to get the expressed permission of the system administrator before you attempt to hack their system.

It is best you get their permission in writing so you are able to have solid proof you had permission to break into their system.

Chapter Seven:
Starting Techniques for Using Python

When you first open Python, you will see a bunch of lines of codes. This will either be the coding you have created yourself or it will be the coding that has been inputted into Python.

The first thing you will do to program while using Python is to have it type back the words you send into it. The ">>>" you see is what the program directs you to type for your codes and commands. When you type "print Hello World, SLUAST" for example, it will come back without the quotation marks.

```
Python 2.7.12 Shell                                    —   □   ×

File  Edit  Shell  Debug  Options  Window  Help
Python 2.7.12 (v2.7.12:d33e0cf91556, Jun 27 2016, 15:19:22) [MSC v.1500 32 bit (
Intel)] on win32
Type "copyright", "credits" or "license()" for more information.
>>> print "Hello World, SLUAST"
Hello World, SLUAST
>>> |


                                                                      Ln: 5  Col: 4
```

It always helps for you to know the basics, such as knowing that if you type print, it can be sent back to you.

The awesome thing about Python is that it can also act as your calculator. When you "print 5", you will just get the number.

However, should you enter "print 5+22" you will get "27" as the response.

Now, let's move it just a step forward and enter a word phrase with strings and numbers.

If you enter "print "im elite," +1337", you will get an error code that looks like this:

Traceback (most recent call last):

File "<pyshell#6>", line 1, in <module>

print "im elite"+1337

TypeError: cannot concatenate 'str' and 'int' objects

```
Python 2.7.12 Shell                                    —    □    ×

File  Edit  Shell  Debug  Options  Window  Help

Python 2.7.12 (v2.7.12:d33e0cf91556, Jun 27 2016, 15:19:22) [MSC v.1500 32 bit
(Intel)] on win32
Type "copyright", "credits" or "license()" for more information.
>>> print "im elite," + 1337

Traceback (most recent call last):
  File "<pyshell#0>", line 1, in <module>
    print "im elite," + 1337
TypeError: cannot concatenate 'str' and 'int' objects
>>> |

                                                        Ln: 9  Col: 4
```

Where you see the word "file" is to say which file and where the error in the file is located. Then it will show the code, and a little brief description of the error. This is an error where you cannot add strings to integers.

Luckily, the coding you can do with language programs is flexible; you just have to solve around it like the other programmers do. To solve this particular error, you can turn the user you want to use into a variable. Just like when you do regular math, X is going to be your placeholder. Therefore, let us say that X is 1337 then you are going to enter "print "im elite" + X and do not hit enter. If you do, you will receive the same error code you just got.

Since you have not yet changed the variables X's number which is 1337 ito a string by connecting quotation marks (") and apostrophes (') together like the following code:

X= '1337'

Print "im elite" + X

Then your final result will read:

Im elite 1337

Now you should not have received an error code.

Dict/Set Comprehensions

It is very possible that you know about list comprehensions, but just because you know of those, you may not be aware of the dict/set comprehensions that you can create using Python.

Dicts and sets are easy to use and just as effective as a list comprehension.

An example would be:

*my_dict = {i: i * i for i in xrange(10)}*

my_set = {i * 15 for i in xrange(10)}

```
Python 2.7.12 Shell                                      —    □    ×
File  Edit  Shell  Debug  Options  Window  Help
Python 2.7.12 (v2.7.12:d33e0cf91556, Jun 27 2016, 15:19:22) [MSC v.1500 32 bit (
Intel)] on win32
Type "copyright", "credits" or "license()" for more information.
>>> my_dict = {i: i * i for i in xrange(10)}
>>> print "my_dict: ", my_dict
my_dict:  {0: 0, 1: 1, 2: 4, 3: 9, 4: 16, 5: 25, 6: 36, 7: 49, 8: 64, 9: 81}
>>> my_set = {i * 15 for i in xrange(10)}
>>> print "my_set: ", my_set
my_set:  set([0, 135, 105, 75, 45, 15, 120, 90, 60, 30])
>>> |
                                                              Ln: 9  Col: 4
```

There is only a difference of ':' in both

Forcing Float Division

Now going back to the mathematics you can do using Python. You can divide numbers using the backslash key. Normally, division will always give you a whole number answer. For Python 2, you will have to do something like this:

Result=1.0/2

However, there is a trick you can use to forgo the .0.

from __future__ import division
result = ½
 # print(result)
 # 0.5

However, you will not have to worry about this if you are using Python 3 as it is automatically handled by Python.

Chapter Eight:
Techniques and Strategies

Even though Python is easy to use, there are still things you can do to make using it slightly easier for you to use it. Some will make writing your coding slightly easier for you to get through it quicker.

Four Types of Quotes

Python will allow you to put both double quotations and single quotes. This will come in handy when coming from another language since everyone puts a double or single quote for different things. Python will not allow you to interchange the quotes, if you start with one, you must end with the same one.

However, Python will enable you to be able to put two or more types of quotes. Quotes like triple quotes are created by typing three single quotes.

A triple-double quote is created when you type three double quotes. Using this function enables the programmer to be able to have several layers of quotes without the worry of escaping their quotes.

Example: print """I wish that I'd never heard him say, "'She said, "He said, 'Give me five dollars'"""""

The Truthfulness of Various Objects

If you use Java, Python is false if empty and true if not. In other words, you do not have to check to see if the length of a string, list, tuple, or dict is zero or is equal to an empty one.

Just by checking the truthfulness is enough. Therefore, if you expect the number zero to false, all other numbers are going to be true.

Example: 1my_object='Test'# True example
2# my_object = '' # False example
3
4iflen(my_object)>0:
5print'my_object is not empty'
6
7iflen(my_object):# 0 will evaluate to False
8print'my_object is not empty'
9
10ifmy_object!='':
11print'my_object is not empty'
12
13ifmy_object:# an empty string will evaluate to False
14print'my_object is not empty'

Checking if a String Contains Substring:

When using Python, you can test your list, tuple, or even dict by testing the expression 'item in list' or even by using 'item not in list.'

Example: string='Hi there'# True example
2# string = 'Good bye' # False example
3 ifstring.find('Hi')!=-1:
4print'Success!'

When you use this script, it makes it much simpler and cleaner so you can test what needs to be tested within your script.

How to Pretty Print a List

An average user of a program does not want to see the brackets around everything. So, they would rather see a clean printed list, even if it is obvious what is in the list. The solution for this is to use a string's 'join' method.

Example: 1recent_presidents=['George   Bush','Bill Clinton','George W. Bush']
2print'The   three   most   recent   presidents   were: %s.'%', '.join(recent_presidents)
3# prints 'The three most recent presidents were: George Bush, Bill Clinton, George W. Bush.

```
Python 2.7.12 Shell                                          —   □   ×
File  Edit  Shell  Debug  Options  Window  Help
Python 2.7.12 (v2.7.12:d33e0cf91556, Jun 27 2016, 15:19:22) [MSC v.1500 32 bit (Intel)] on win32
Type "copyright", "credits" or "license()" for more information.
>>> recent_presidents = ['George Bush', 'Bill Clinton', 'George W. Bush']
>>> print 'The three most recent presidents were: %s.' % ', '.join(recent_presidents)
The three most recent presidents were: George Bush, Bill Clinton, George W. Bush.
>>> |
                                                             Ln: 6  Col: 4
```

When you use the join method, it will turn the list into a casting of each item into a string and connect them with the string that join was called on. Python program is smart enough not to put one after the last element.

An extra bonus would be that Python runs in linear time. Do not try and create a string by adding '+'ing. Instead, list the items together in for a loop. This will keep your list from being ugly although it takes more time.

Float Division vs Integers

When dividing an integer by another will give you a truncated result into an integer. For example, 5/2 will then give you a return of 2.

The first solution to fixing this is to turn one of the integers into a float. That way if the values happen to be static, you will just append a .0 to make one float. So, 5.0/2 will then give you 2.5 instead of just 2. Another way you can do this is to cast one of the values.

A second solution would give you a cleaner code, but you need to remember that your code will not need to rely on truncation. If you do a from_future_import division while working with Python, you will always get the result of a float while doing division. Just as 5/2 will give you 2.5. However, you will need to truncate the integer somewhere, use the // operation.

Example: 15/2# Returns 2
25.0/2# Returns 2.5
3float(5)/2# Returns 2.5
45//2# Returns 2
5
6from__future__importdivision
75/2# Returns 2.5
85.0/2# Returns 2.5
9float(5)/2# Returns 2.5
105//2# Returns 2

The point float division will become the default. Should you want your code to future-proof, you will need to use the // operation. If you want the truncating division, you will need to use the from_future_import division.

Lambda Functions

When coding, sometimes, you will want to do a short complex operation multiple times or to pass a function as an argument. To do this, you can use the lambda function or you can use your function the normal way. A lambda function is a mini function that will give you the result as a single expression.

Example: 1defadd(a,b):returna+b
2
3add2=lambdaa,b:a+b

When using the lambda function, the expression can be used within another statement. For example, should you want to use the map functions, a function will be called on every element in your list and therefore you get the results of the list.

Example: 1squares=map(lambdaa:a*a,[1,2,3,4,5])
2# squares is now [1,4,9,16,25]

```
Python 2.7.12 Shell                                  —   □   X
File  Edit  Shell  Debug  Options  Window  Help
Python 2.7.12 (v2.7.12:d33e0cf91556, Jun 27 2016, 15:19:22) [MSC v.1500 32 bit (
Intel)] on win32
Type "copyright", "credits" or "license()" for more information.
>>> map(lambda a: a*a, [1,2,3,4,5])
[1, 4, 9, 16, 25]
>>>
                                                        Ln: 5  Col: 4
```

If you don't use lambda, you will then result in having to define your own functions every time you use them. And you will have to define them separately every time. Using lambda saves a line of code and the variable name.

Syntax for lambda functions. Variables are defined as a comma separated list of variables that your function can receive. If you are unable to use the keywords, you will not want to put these in parentheses. Expressions are going to be defined as an inline Python expression. Expressions are what the function is going to return.

Mapping the List

When attempting to square everything on your list, it may look a little something like this:

```
1numbers=[1,2,3,4,5]
2squares=[]
3fornumberinnumbers:
4squares.append(number*number)
5# Now, squares should have [1,4,9,16,25]
```

In doing this, you have essentially "mapped" from one list to another, but, you can still use the map function to make your code look like this:

```
1numbers=[1,2,3,4,5]
2squares=map(lambdax:x*x,numbers)
3# Now, squares should have [1,4,9,16,25]
```

```
Python 2.7.12 Shell                                         —    □    ×
File  Edit  Shell  Debug  Options  Window  Help
Python 2.7.12 (v2.7.12:d33e0cf91556, Jun 27 2016, 15:19:22) [MSC v.1500 32 bit (Intel)
] on win32
Type "copyright", "credits" or "license()" for more information.
>>> numbers = [1,2,3,4,5]
>>> squares = map(lambda x: x*x, numbers)# Now, squares should have [1,4,9,16,25]
>>> print squares
[1, 4, 9, 16, 25]
>>> |
                                                            Ln: 7  Col: 4
```

Basically, you have done the same thing with two commands and now made your code shorter. Tis makes it harder to tell what map function is when you glance at it. However, it accepts the function and applies it to the list and every element in your list. When using mapping, it will still look messy. One way to make your list look cleaner is to use a list comprehension.

In doing this, your list will now look like this:

```
1numbers=[1,2,3,4,5]
2squares=map(lambdax:x*x,numbers)
3# Now, squares should have [1,4,9,16,25]
```

Doing this is the exact same thing as the first wo examples, however, the biggest difference is that the code is now shorter and cleaner looking. This will help make it to where no one has any problem in determining what it does, no matter if they know how Python works or not.

Filtering Your List

Your list is now done, and now you want to filter that list to find a specific item. For example, what if you want to remove every element with a value that is equal to or greater than four? Someone who is new to Python might write their code to look like this:

```
1numbers=[1,2,3,4,5]
2numbers_under_4=[]
3fornumberinnumbers:
4ifnumber<4:
5numbers_under_4.append(number)
6# Now, numbers_under_4 contains [1,4,9]
```

The code looks simple enough, but it is too long when you could shorten it. Writing the code out this way took four lines, appending to do something completely trivial and took two degrees of nesting. To reduce the size of the code, you will need to use the filter function. In using this function, your code will look like this:

```
1numbers=[1,2,3,4,5]
2numbers_under_4=filter(lambdax:x<4,numbers)
3# Now, numbers_under_4 contains [1,2,3]
```

Just like when you use the map function, the filter function reduces the code size and makes the code look rather ugly. But because the map and filter functions are similar. You can use the list comprehension function so every element in your list is evaluated and makes the code look prettier just like we did when using the mapping function. In doing this, the code will now look like this:

```
1numbers=[1,2,3,4,5]
2numbers_under_4=[numberfornumberinnumbersifnumber<4]
3# Now, numbers_under_4 contains [1,2,3]
```

Now your code is not only shorter, but it is cleaner and easier to understand.

Mapping and Filtering at Once

Hopefully at this point in time you now understand the concept of how to use the list comprehension function. Ultimately, this has hopefully convinced you that using the map and filter functions are nothing but a waste of your time.

You can use the filter and map function at the same time. This will give you the squares of each element in your list and any element that is under the equivalence of four. Someone who is new to coding would probably write their code out to look simply like this:

```
1numbers=[1,2,3,4,5]
2squares=[]
3fornumberinnumbers:
4ifnumber<4:
5squares.append(number*number)
6# squares is now [1,4,9]
```

```
Python 2.7.12 Shell                                              —    □    ×

File  Edit  Shell  Debug  Options  Window  Help
Python 2.7.12 (v2.7.12:d33e0cf91556, Jun 27 2016, 15:19:22) [MSC v.1500 32 bit (
Intel)] on win32
Type "copyright", "credits" or "license()" for more information.
>>> numbers = [1,2,3,4,5]
>>> squares = []
>>> for number in numbers:
        if number < 4:
            squares.append(number*number) # squares is now [1,4,9]

>>> print squares
[1, 4, 9]
>>>
                                                                   Ln: 12  Col: 4
```

The good thing about this code is that instead of being horizontal, it is looking more and more vertical. But, we still want our code to be simplified. This is where we would attempt to use the map and filter functions. Doing this command would cause the code to come out looking something like this:

```
1numbers=[1,2,3,4,5]
2squares=map(lambdax:x*x,filter(lambdax:x<4,numbers))
3# squares is now [1,4,9]
```

Just as before, our code looks ugly and is unreadable to other coders. So, let's try and use the list comprehension. When using this command, our code now looks like this:

```
1numbers=[1,2,3,4,5]
2squares=[number*numberfornumberinnumbersifnumber<4
]
3# square is now [1,4,9]
```

When using the list comprehension, once again the code is now readable and shorter than it was before and cleaner looking. It is better than using the map and filter functions separately and having to make your code pretty twice instead of just once.

List comprehension filters and then maps your list for you to give you a cleaner look and also it cuts out the functions that will ultimately have you using the list comprehension function anyways.

Generator Expressions

While list comprehensions make things easier while coding, they also have their downside as well. The biggest downside is that list comprehension stores the entire list in the memory at once. While working with smaller lists, this isn't such a problem. It's not even a problem if you have several small lists. But, eventually you'll be making more work for yourself and therefore your method will be pretty inefficient.

The newest function in Python 2.4 is the generator expressions. The best thing about the generator expressions is that it does not load the entire list into the memory at once. Instead, the generator will create a generator object so only one element in the list is loaded at a time.

Unfortunately, if you need the entire list for something, using a generator will not be the best option. If you are just passing your list off to something that will take any iterable object, then you can just use the generator function.

Most generator expressions use the same syntax as the list comprehensions but use parentheses instead of brackets. This is what a generated expression code would look like

```
1numbers=(1,2,3,4,5)# Since we're going for efficiency, I'm using a tuple instead of a list ;)
2squares_under_10=(number*numberfornumberinnumbersif number*number<10)
3# squares_under_10 is now a generator object, from which each successive value can be gotten by calling .next()
4
5forsquareinsquares_under_10:
6printsquare,
7# prints '1 4 9'
```

A generated expression is more efficient than using a list comprehension.

If you want to use the generated expressions for many items, you'll only be able to see one item on the list at a time. In the case that you need the entire list at once, you'll need to use the list comprehensions function. Unless your list is too big, using the generator expressions is a good option to use. Otherwise, you're not going to see any difference in the efficiency.

Generator expressions only use one set of parentheses. While calling a function with only the generator function, you will need to use parentheses. That would look something like this: some_function(item for item in list).

Nested 'for' statements

You can create rather complex lists if you use the list comprehension and generator expressions. But, you will not only be able to map ad filter, you will also be able to nest the for expressions. Once again, someone new to Python might write their code out like this

```
1forxin(0,1,2,3):
2foryin(0,1,2,3):
3ifx<y:
4print(x,y,x*y),
5
6# prints (0, 1, 0) (0, 2, 0) (0, 3, 0) (1, 2, 2) (1, 3, 3) (2, 3, 6)
```

Much like a lot of our codes that we've given you examples of, this code is messy and hard to understand. Using the list comprehension function you can take your code from that, to this

```
1print[(x,y,x*y)forxin(0,1,2,3)foryin(0,1,2,3)ifx<y]
2# prints [(0, 1, 0), (0, 2, 0), (0, 3, 0), (1, 2, 2), (1, 3, 3), (2, 3, 6)]
```

This code iterates over four values of y and each value over the four values of x and then filters and maps it. Each item on the list is a list of x, y, x * y.

Notice that the xrange (4) has a lot cleaner of a look than the one that uses (0, 1, 2, 3).

Syntax for List Comprehensions and Generator Expressions

A list is defined as any series of items.

Variables are defined as variables that are assigned to the current list elements, very similar to the regular for loop.

Condition is defined as an inline Python expression. This includes the local scope and variables. If it is evaluated as true, it will be included in the result.

Element is defined as another inline Python expression but includes the local scope and variables. The actual element will be included in the result.

Chapter Nine:
Different Versions of Python

There are multiple versions of Python because of the development that has happened to Python therefore making it to where there are multiple versions. Not only that, but each version has different aspects of it that can be helpful in your coding experience.

Version 1.0

By January of 1994, Python version 1.0 was released. The new features included in this version were the functional programming tools of lambda, map, filter and the reduce command. When asked, Van Rossum stated that the new functions that Python had acquired were courtesy of a Lisp hacker that missed them and submitted the working patches.

While still working with CWI Python version 1.2 was released in '95. Even after that, Rossum continued to work on Python as he worked with CNRI (Corporation for National Research Initiatives). It was here that he would end up releasing several new versions of Python.

Version 1.4 was released and more new features were added to Python. Among the new changes were the modula3 that had inspired the keyword arguments and the built in support that allowed Python users to use complex numbers. There was also a basic form of data hiding by name mangling which was earlier bypassed.

Rossum launched the CP4E while he was working at CNRI. CP4E is known as Computer Programming for Everyone. It was initially intended to make programming easier for people with basic knowledge in programming languages. Since it had a clean syntax, Python served as a central role in CP4E. DARPA funded the CP4E projects.

Finally, when 2007 came around, the CP4E project was inactive because Python now contacted the non-programmers.

BeOpen

BeOpen.com was created by the Python development teach to create BeOpen in 2000. CNRI pressured the release of Python version 1.6 to where the Python development team left. Version 1.6 was not released due to it overlapping the release of version 2.0.

Version 2.0 was the only release to come from BeOpen.com. once Python 2.0 was released, the Python development team and Van Rossum joined digital creations.

Now, version 1.6 did not get released to include a new CNRI license that was longer than the CWI license that was used with earlier releases. The new license had a clause that was placed within it stating that it was governed by the laws of the State of Virginia. Because of this, the Free Software Foundation fought for the choice of law clause. BeOpen, CNRI and FSF soon negotiated that Python's free software license be made GPL compatible.

Because of this, version 1.6.1 was released but some of the bugs from 1.6 were fixed as well as having the new license.

Version 2.0

Version 2.0 was released with the list comprehensions function. This function was borrowed from the languages of SETL and Haskell. Python's syntax was similarly written to Haskell's program, however did not include the punctuation that Haskell seemed to prefer. Python preferred the alphabetic keywords. 2.0 also had a garbage collection that would allow the system to collect reference cycles.

Just as with version 1.6.1, version 2.1 had its license renamed Python Software Foundation License. Because of this, all the codes and documentation with specifications were added at the time of Python 2.1's alpha release. 2.1 was owned by the Python Software Foundation which was a non-profit organization that happened to form in 2001. With the change to the language specifications, the release had to include the support of nested scopes and other statically scoped languages.

With version 2.2, all of Python's types were now written in C and the classes were put into one hierarchy. The single unification that Python made was purely object oriented. As well as this being changed, the generators were also added that were inspired by Icon.

In November of 2014, Python then announced the release of version 2.7 would be in 2020. With this news, it was confirmed there would no longer be a Python version 2.8 and any Python users would be expected to move to Python 3.4+ as soon as possible.

Version 3.0

Version 3.0 was called Python 3000 or Py3K. This was created to help rectify some of the more fundamental design flaws in the languages of the previous versions. Although, some changes that the development team wanted were not kept and Python being able to retain the backwards compatibility with the 2.x series.

Basically, Python 3 was created to reduce the feature duplications and remove some of the old ways of doing things and making things easier for the Python users.

Chapter Ten:
Python Codes

While Python coding is simple to read, this is one of the best programming languages you can use while you are writing out your coding. Some of the following codes are codes that you are going to want to know when you are writing out your codes.

Unpacking

```
>>>a,b,c=1,2,3
>>>a,b,c
(1, 2, 3)
>>>a,b,c=[1,2,3]
>>>a,b,c
(1, 2, 3)
>>>a,b,c=(2*i+1foriinrange(3))
>>>a,b,c
(1, 3, 5)
>>>a,(b,c),d=[1,(2,3),4]
>>>a
1
>>>b
2
>>>c
3
>>>d
4
```

Unpacking for swapping variables:

```
>>>a,b=1,2
>>>a,b=b,a
>>>a,b
(2, 1)
```

Extended unpacking (use in Python 3 only)

```
>>>a,*b,c=[1,2,3,4,5]
>>>a
1
>>>b
[2, 3, 4]
>>>c
5
```

Negative indexing

```
>>>a=[0,1,2,3,4,5,6,7,8,9,10]
>>>a[-1]
10
>>>a[-3]
8
```

List slices (a[start: end])

```
>>>a=[0,1,2,3,4,5,6,7,8,9,10]
>>>a[2:8]
[2, 3, 4, 5, 6, 7]
```

List Slices with Negative Indexing

```
>>>a=[0,1,2,3,4,5,6,7,8,9,10]
>>>a[-4:-2]
[7, 8]
```

List Slices with Step (a[start: end: step])

```
>>>a=[0,1,2,3,4,5,6,7,8,9,10]
>>>a[::2]
[0, 2, 4, 6, 8, 10]
>>>a[::3]
[0, 3, 6, 9]
>>>a[2:8:2]
[2, 4, 6]
```

List Slices with negative step

```
>>>a=[0,1,2,3,4,5,6,7,8,9,10]
>>>a[::-1]
[10, 9, 8, 7, 6, 5, 4, 3, 2, 1, 0]
>>>a[::-2]
[10, 8, 6, 4, 2, 0]
```

List Slice Assignment

```
>>>a=[1,2,3,4,5]
>>>a[2:3]=[0,0]
>>>a
[1, 2, 0, 0, 4, 5]
>>>a[1:1]=[8,9]
>>>a
[1, 8, 9, 2, 0, 0, 4, 5]
>>>a[1:-1]=[]
>>>a
[1, 5]
```

Naming Slices (slice(start, end, step))

```
>>>a=[0,1,2,3,4,5]
>>>LASTTHREE=slice(-3,None)
>>>LASTTHREE
slice(-3, None, None)
>>>a[LASTTHREE]
[3, 4, 5]
```

Iterating over list index and value pairs (enumerate)

```
>>>a=['Hello','world','!']
>>>fori,xinenumerate(a):
... print'{}: {}'.format(i,x)
...
0: Hello
1: world
2: !
```

Iterating over dictionary key and value pairs (dict.iteritems)

```
>>>m={'a':1,'b':2,'c':3,'d':4}
>>>fork,vinm.iteritems():
... print'{}: {}'.format(k,v)
...
a: 1
c: 3
b: 2
d: 4
```

Zipping and unzipping lists and iterables

```
>>>a=[1,2,3]
>>>b=['a','b','c']
>>>z=zip(a,b)
>>>z
[(1, 'a'), (2, 'b'), (3, 'c')]
>>>zip(*z)
[(1, 2, 3), ('a', 'b', 'c')]
```

Grouping adjacent list items using zip

```
>>>a=[1,2,3,4,5,6]
>>># Using iterators
>>>group_adjacent=lambdaa,k:zip(*([iter(a)]*k))
>>>group_adjacent(a,3)
[(1, 2, 3), (4, 5, 6)]
>>>group_adjacent(a,2)
[(1, 2), (3, 4), (5, 6)]
>>>group_adjacent(a,1)
[(1,), (2,), (3,), (4,), (5,), (6,)]

>>># Using slices
>>>fromitertoolsimportislice
>>>group_adjacent=lambdaa,k:zip(*(islice(a,i,None,k)foriinr
ange(k)))
>>>group_adjacent(a,3)
[(1, 2, 3), (4, 5, 6)]
>>>group_adjacent(a,2)
[(1, 2), (3, 4), (5, 6)]
>>>group_adjacent(a,1)
[(1,), (2,), (3,), (4,), (5,), (6,)]
```

Sliding windows (n-grams) using zip and iterators

```
>>>fromitertoolsimportislice
>>>defn_grams(a,n):
... z=(islice(a,i,None)foriinrange(n))
... returnzip(*z)
...
>>>a=[1,2,3,4,5,6]
>>>n_grams(a,3)
[(1, 2, 3), (2, 3, 4), (3, 4, 5), (4, 5, 6)]
>>>n_grams(a,2)
[(1, 2), (2, 3), (3, 4), (4, 5), (5, 6)]
>>>n_grams(a,4)
[(1, 2, 3, 4), (2, 3, 4, 5), (3, 4, 5, 6)]
```

Inverting a dictionary using zip

```
>>>m={'a':1,'b':2,'c':3,'d':4}
>>>m.items()
[('a', 1), ('c', 3), ('b', 2), ('d', 4)]
>>>zip(m.values(),m.keys())
[(1, 'a'), (3, 'c'), (2, 'b'), (4, 'd')]
>>>mi=dict(zip(m.values(),m.keys()))
>>>mi
{1: 'a', 2: 'b', 3: 'c', 4: 'd'}
```

Flattening lists

```
>>>a=[[1,2],[3,4],[5,6]]
>>>list(itertools.chain.from_iterable(a))
[1, 2, 3, 4, 5, 6]

>>>sum(a,[])
[1, 2, 3, 4, 5, 6]

>>>[xforlinaforxinl]
[1, 2, 3, 4, 5, 6]
>>>a=[[[1,2],[3,4]],[[5,6],[7,8]]]
>>>[xforl1inaforl2inl1forxinl2]
[1, 2, 3, 4, 5, 6, 7, 8]

>>>a=[1,2,[3,4],[[5,6],[7,8]]]
>>>flatten=lambdax:[yforlinxforyinflatten(l)]iftype(x)islistelse[x]
>>>flatten(a)
[1, 2, 3, 4, 5, 6, 7, 8]
```

Generator expressions

```
>>>g=(x**2 for x in xrange(10))
>>>next(g)
0
>>>next(g)
1
>>>next(g)
4
>>>next(g)
9
>>>sum(x**3 for x in xrange(10))
2025
>>>sum(x**3 for x in xrange(10) if x%3==1)
408
```

Dictionary comprehensions

```
>>>m={x:x**2 for x in range(5)}
>>>m
{0: 0, 1: 1, 2: 4, 3: 9, 4: 16}

>>>m={x:'A'+str(x) for x in range(10)}
>>>m
{0: 'A0', 1: 'A1', 2: 'A2', 3: 'A3', 4: 'A4', 5: 'A5', 6: 'A6', 7: 'A7', 8:
'A8', 9: 'A9'}
```

Inverting a dictionary using a dictionary comprehension

```
>>>m={'a':1,'b':2,'c':3,'d':4}
>>>m
{'d': 4, 'a': 1, 'b': 2, 'c': 3}
>>>{v:kfork,vinm.items()}
{1: 'a', 2: 'b', 3: 'c', 4: 'd'}
```

Named tuples (collections . namedtuple)

```
>>>Point=collections.namedtuple('Point',['x','y'])
>>>p=Point(x=1.0,y=2.0)
>>>p
Point(x=1.0, y=2.0)
>>>p.x
1.0
>>>p.w
2.0
```

Inheriting from named tuples

```
>>>classPoint(collections.namedtuple('PointBase',['x','y'])):
... __slots__=()
... def__add__(self,other):
... returnPoint(x=self.x+other.x,y=self.y+other.y)
...
>>>p=Point(x=1.0,y=2.0)
>>>q=Point(x=2.0,y=3.0)
>>>p+q
Point(x=3.0, y=5.0)
```

Sets and set operations

```
>>>A={1,2,3,3}
>>>A
set([1, 2, 3])
>>>B={3,4,5,6,7}
>>>B
set([3, 4, 5, 6, 7])
>>>A|B
set([1, 2, 3, 4, 5, 6, 7])
>>>A&B
set([3])
>>>A-B
set([1, 2])
>>>B-A
set([4, 5, 6, 7])
>>>A^B
set([1, 2, 4, 5, 6, 7])
>>>(A^B)==((A-B)|(B-A))
True
```

Multisets and multiset operations (collections.counter)

```
>>>A=collections.Counter([1,2,2])
>>>B=collections.Counter([2,2,3])
>>>A
Counter({2: 2, 1: 1})
>>>B
Counter({2: 2, 3: 1})
>>>A|B
Counter({2: 2, 1: 1, 3: 1})
>>>A&B
Counter({2: 2})
>>>A+B
Counter({2: 4, 1: 1, 3: 1})
>>>A-B
Counter({1: 1})
>>>B-A
Counter({3: 1})
```

Most common elements in an iterable (collections.counter)

```
>>>A=collections.Counter([1,1,2,2,3,3,3,3,4,5,6,7])
>>>A
Counter({3: 4, 1: 2, 2: 2, 4: 1, 5: 1, 6: 1, 7: 1})
>>>A.most_common(1)
[(3, 4)]
>>>A.most_common(3)
[(3, 4), (1, 2), (2, 2)]
```

Double ended queue (collections.deque)

```
>>>Q=collections.deque()
>>>Q.append(1)
>>>Q.appendleft(2)
>>>Q.extend([3,4])
>>>Q.extendleft([5,6])
>>>Q
deque([6, 5, 2, 1, 3, 4])
>>>Q.pop()
4
>>>Q.popleft()
6
>>>Q
deque([5, 2, 1, 3])
>>>Q.rotate(3)
>>>Q
deque([2, 1, 3, 5])
>>>Q.rotate(-3)
>>>Q
deque([5, 2, 1, 3])
```

Double ended queue with maximum length (collections.deque)

```
>>>last_three=collections.deque(maxlen=3)
>>>foriinxrange(10):
... last_three.append(i)
... print', '.join(str(x)forxinlast_three)
...
0
0, 1
0, 1, 2
1, 2, 3
2, 3, 4
3, 4, 5
4, 5, 6
5, 6, 7
6, 7, 8
7, 8, 9
```

Ordered dictionaries (collections.OrderedDict)

```
>>>m=dict((str(x),x)forxinrange(10))
>>>print', '.join(m.keys())
1, 0, 3, 2, 5, 4, 7, 6, 9, 8
>>>m=collections.OrderedDict((str(x),x)forxinrange(10))
>>>print', '.join(m.keys())
0, 1, 2, 3, 4, 5, 6, 7, 8, 9
>>>m=collections.OrderedDict((str(x),x)forxinrange(10,0,-1))
>>>print', '.join(m.keys())
10, 9, 8, 7, 6, 5, 4, 3, 2, 1
```

Default dictionaries (collections.defaultdict)

```
>>>m=dict()
>>>m['a']
Traceback (most recent call last):
 File "<stdin>", line 1, in <module>
KeyError: 'a'
>>>
>>>m=collections.defaultdict(int)
>>>m['a']
0
>>>m['b']
0
>>>m=collections.defaultdict(str)
>>>m['a']
"
>>>m['b']+='a'
>>>m['b']
'a'
>>>m=collections.defaultdict(lambda:'[default value]')
>>>m['a']
'[default value]'
>>>m['b']
'[default value]'
```

Using default dictionaries to represent simple trees

```
>>>importjson
>>>tree=lambda:collections.defaultdict(tree)
>>>root=tree()
>>>root['menu']['id']='file'
>>>root['menu']['value']='File'
>>>root['menu']['menuitems']['new']['value']='New'
>>>root['menu']['menuitems']['new']['onclick']='new();'
>>>root['menu']['menuitems']['open']['value']='Open'
>>>root['menu']['menuitems']['open']['onclick']='open();'
>>>root['menu']['menuitems']['close']['value']='Close'
>>>root['menu']['menuitems']['close']['onclick']='close();'
>>>printjson.dumps(root,sort_keys=True,indent=4,separators=(',',': '))
{
    "menu": {
        "id": "file",
        "menuitems": {
            "close": {
                "onclick": "close();",
                "value": "Close"
            },
            "new": {
                "onclick": "new();",
                "value": "New"
            },
            "open": {
                "onclick": "open();",
                "value": "Open"
            }
        },
```

```
    "value": "File"
  }
}
```

Mapping objects to unique counting numbers (collections.defaultdict)

```
>>>importitertools,collections
>>>value_to_numeric_map=collections.defaultdict(itertools.
count().next)
>>>value_to_numeric_map['a']
0
>>>value_to_numeric_map['b']
1
>>>value_to_numeric_map['c']
2
>>>value_to_numeric_map['a']
0
>>>value_to_numeric_map['b']
1
```

Largest and smallest elements (heapq.nlargest and heapq.nsmallest)

```
>>>a=[random.randint(0,100)for__inxrange(100)]
>>>heapq.nsmallest(5,a)
[3, 3, 5, 6, 8]
>>>heapq.nlargest(5,a)
[100, 100, 99, 98, 98]
```

Cartesian products (itertools.product)

```
>>>forpinitertools.product([1,2,3],[4,5]):
(1, 4)
(1, 5)
(2, 4)
(2, 5)
(3, 4)
(3, 5)
>>>forpinitertools.product([0,1],repeat=4):
... print''.join(str(x)forxinp)
...
0000
0001
0010
0011
0100
0101
0110
0111
1000
1001
1010
1011
1100
1101
1110
1111
```

Combinations and combinations with replacement (itertools.combinations and itertools.combinations_with_replacement)

```
>>>forcinitertools.combinations([1,2,3,4,5],3):
... print''.join(str(x)forxinc)
...
123
124
125
134
135
145
234
235
245
345
>>>forcinitertools.combinations_with_replacement([1,2,3],2)
:
... print''.join(str(x)forxinc)
...
11
12
13
22
23
33
```

Permutations (itertools.permutations)

```
>>>forpinitertools.permutations([1,2,3,4]):
... print"".join(str(x)forxinp)
...
1234
1243
1324
1342
1423
1432
2134
2143
2314
2341
2413
2431
3124
3142
3214
3241
3412
3421
4123
4132
4213
4231
4312
4321
```

Chaining iterables (itertools.chain)

```
>>>a=[1,2,3,4]
>>>forpinitertools.chain(itertools.combinations(a,2),itertools.
combinations(a,3)):
... printp
...
(1, 2)
(1, 3)
(1, 4)
(2, 3)
(2, 4)
(3, 4)
(1, 2, 3)
(1, 2, 4)
(1, 3, 4)
(2, 3, 4)
>>>forsubsetinitertools.chain.from_iterable(itertools.combin
ations(a,n)forninrange(len(a)+1))
... printsubset
...
()
(1,)
(2,)
(3,)
(4,)
(1, 2)
(1, 3)
(1, 4)
(2, 3)
(2, 4)
(3, 4)
(1, 2, 3)
```

(1, 2, 4)
(1, 3, 4)
(2, 3, 4)
(1, 2, 3, 4)

Chapter Eleven:
Python References

These are the following references that you can use for you to find different things you may need when learning how to use Python.

www.computerhope.com/unix/python.htm

www.computerhope.com/jargon/p/proglang.htm

www.docs.python-guide.org/en/latest

www.pythontips.com/2015/04/19/nifty-python-tricks/

www.sinister.ly/thread-python-tutorial-beginners-1

www.codeacademy.com/articles/glossary-python

www.pythonhow.com/building-a-website-with-python-flask/

Conclusion

Thank you again for purchasing this book! We greatly appreciate it!

I hope this book was able to help you in learning the basics of how you can use Python for all your coding needs.

The next step is for you to download Python and to start learning the ins and outs of writing out your own code for whatever it is you are wanting to write code out for.

Finally, if you enjoyed this book, please take the time to share your thoughts and post a review on Amazon. It would be greatly appreciated!

Thank you and good luck on your journey of writing code by using Python.

For Updates on

New Releases & Book Promotions

Subscribe to our mailing list at

www.AshPublishing.net

Glossary

As you have seen by reading this book, Python has multiple commands and options. The terms below are the ones that you will need to know as you are learning how to write out your own code for using Python.

Class

Python supports the object oriented programming paradigm. Much like other OOP languages, Python has different classes defined by wireframes of different objects. A class may have subclasses but may only inherit directly from one superclass.

Syntax:

```
classClassName(object):
"""This is a class"""
   class_variable
def__init__(self,*args):
    self.args = args
def__repr__(self):
return"Something to represent the object as a string"
defother_method(self,*args):
# do something else
```

Example:

```
classHorse(object):
"""Horse represents a Horse"""
   species = "Equus ferus caballus"
def__init__(self,color,weight,wild=False):
    self.color = color
    self.weight = weight
    self.wild = wild
def__repr__(self):
return"%s horse weighing %f and wild status is %b" % (self.color,self.weight,self.wild)
defmake_sound(self):
print"neighhhh"
```

```
defmovement(self):
return"walk"
```

Syntax:

```
classClassName(SuperClass):
# same as above
# use 'super' keyword to get from above
```

Example:

```
classRaceHorse(Horse):
"""A faster horse that inherits from Horse"""
defmovement(self):
return"run"
defmovement_slow(self):
return super(Horse,self).movement()
def__repr__(self):
return"%s race horse weighing %f and wild status is %b"
(self.color,self.weight,self.wild)
```

```
>> horse3 = RaceHorse("white",200)
>>print horse3.movement_slow()
"walk"
>>print horse3.movement()
"run"
```

Comments

Single Line Comments: this is augmenting code in which human readable descriptions can help with document design decisions.

Example: # this is a single line comment.
Multi-line Comments: these comments span several lines. You need to use this if you have over four lines of single comments in a row.

Example:
'''

this is
a multi-line
comment, i am handy for commenting out whole
chunks of code very fast
'''

Dictionaries

These are Python's built-in associative data type. The dictionary comprises different key-value pairs where each key corresponds with a different value. Much like sets, dictionaries are unordered.

The keys must be immutable and hashable so the value can be any type. The most common examples of these keys are tuples, numbers, and strings. One dictionary can contain the key types of varying values and varying types.

Syntax:

dict() #createsnewemptydictionary
{}#createsnewemptydictionary

Example:

```
>>my_dict = {}
>>content_of_value1 = "abcd"
>>content_of_value2 = "wxyz"
>>my_dict.update({"key_name1":content_of_value1})
>>my_dict.update({"key_name2":content_of_value2})
>>my_dict
{'key_name2':"wxyz", 'key_name1':"abcd"}
>>my_dict.get("key_name2")
"wxyz"
```

```
Python 2.7.12 Shell                                    —    □    ×
File  Edit  Shell  Debug  Options  Window  Help
Python 2.7.12 (v2.7.12:d33e0cf91556, Jun 27 2016, 15:19:22) [MSC v.1500 32 bit ( ▲
Intel)] on win32
Type "copyright", "credits" or "license()" for more information.
>>> my_dict = {}
>>> content_of_value1 = "abcd"
>>> content_of_value2 = "wxyz"
>>> my_dict.update({"key_name1":content_of_value1})
>>> my_dict.update({"key_name2":content_of_value2})
>>> my_dict
{'key_name2': 'wxyz', 'key_name1': 'abcd'}
>>> my_dict.get("key_name2")
'wxyz'
>>> |
                                                         Ln: 12  Col: 4
```

Syntax:

{key1:value1,key2:value2}

Example:

```
>> my_dict = {"key1":[1,2,3],"key2":"I am a string",123:456}
>> my_dict["key1"] #[1,2,3]
>> my_dict[123] #456
>> my_dict["new key"] = "New value"
>>print my_dict
```
{"key2":"I   am   a   string",   "new   key":"New   value",
"key1":[1,2,3],123:456}

Functions

These functions can be used as abstract pieces of code that can be used elsewhere.

Syntax

```
deffunction_name(parameters):
# Some code here
```

Example

```
defadd_two(a, b):
  c = a + b
return c
```

```
# or without the interim assignment to c
defadd_two(a, b):
return a + b
```

Syntax

```
deffunction_name(parameters,
named_default_parameter=value):
# Some code here
```

Example

```
defshout(exclamation="Hey!"):
print exclamation
```

```
shout() # Displays "Hey!"
```

```
shout("Watch Out!") # Displays "Watch Out!"
```

Function Objects

These are first class objects. This means they can be stored in lists or variables and even can be returned by other functions.

Example

```
# Storing function objects in variables:

defsay_hello(name):
return"Hello, " + name
foo = say_hello("Alice")
# Now the value of 'foo' is "Hello, Alice"

fun = say_hello
# Now the value of 'fun' is a function object we can use like the
original function:
bar = fun("Bob")
# Now the value of 'bar' is "Hello, Bob"
```

Example

```
# Returning functions from functions

# A simple function
defsay_hello(greeter, greeted):
return"Hello, " + greeted + ", I'm " + greeter + "."

# We can use it like this:
print say_hello("Alice", "Bob") # Displays "Hello, Bob, I'm
Alice."

# We can also use it in a function:
defproduce_greeting_from_alice(greeted):
return say_hello("Alice", greeted)
```

```
print produce_greeting_from_alice("Bob") # Displays "Hello,
Bob, I'm Alice."

# We can also return a function from a function by nesting
them:
defproduce_greeting_from(greeter):
defgreet(greeted):
return say_hello(greeter, greeted)
return greet

# Here we create a greeting function for Eve:
produce_greeting_from_eve                              =
produce_greeting_from("Eve")
# 'produce_greeting_from_eve' is now a function:
print produce_greeting_from_eve("Alice") # Displays "Hello,
Alice, I'm Eve."

# You can also invoke the function directly if you want:
print    produce_greeting_from("Bob")("Eve")    #    Displays
"Hello, Eve, I'm Bob."
```

Example

```
# Using functions in a dictionary instead of long if statements:
# Let's say we have a variable called 'current_action' and we
want stuff to happen based on its value:

if current_action == 'PAUSE':
  pause()
elif current_action == 'RESTART':
  restart()
elif current_action == 'RESUME':
  resume()
```

```
# This can get long and complicated if there are many values.
# Instead, we can use a dictionary:

response_dict = {
'PAUSE': pause,
'RESTART': restart,
'RESUME': resume
}

response_dict[current_action]()  # Gets the correct function
from          response_dict        and          calls          it
```

len()

if you use len(some object) it will usually return the number of top-level items that are being queried.

Syntax

len(iterable)

Example

```
>> my_list = [0,4,5,2,3,4,5]
>> len(my_list)
7

>> my_string = 'abcdef'
>> len(my_string)
6
```

List Comprehensions

This is a convenient way to generate or extract information from a list you create

Syntax

[variable for variable in iterable condition]
[variable for variable in iterable]

Example

```
>> x_list = [1,2,3,4,5,6,7]
>> even_list = [num for num in x_list if (num % 2 == 0)]
>> even_list
[2,4,6]

>> m_list = ['AB', 'AC', 'DA', 'FG', 'LB']
>> A_list = [duo for duo in m_list if ('A'in duo)]
>> A_list
['AB', 'AC', 'DA']
```

Lists

This is a data type that orders and holds a collection of values. This can be any type of values. Lists in Python are orders of mutable data types. Unlike tuples, lists can be modified in place or in other words, as you create them.

Example

```
>>x = [1, 2, 3, 4]
>>y = ['spam', 'eggs']
>>x
[1, 2, 3, 4]
```

```
>>y
['spam','eggs']

>>y.append('mash')
>>y
['spam', 'eggs', 'mash']

>>y += ['beans']
>>y
['spam', 'eggs', 'mash', 'beans']
```

Loops

For Loops:

These are clean iteration syntax. The colon and the indentation are usually indicators of for loops.

Example

```
>>for i in range(0, 3):
>>print(i*2)
0
2
4

>> m_list = ["Sir", "Lancelot", "Coconuts"]
>>for item in m_list:
>>print(item)
Sir
Lancelot
Coconuts

>> w_string = "Swift"
>>for letter in w_string:
>>print(letter)
S
w
i
f
t
```

While Loops:

These are permits codes execute repeatedly until a certain condition is met. Usually this is only useful if the number of iterations required is unknown prior to flow entering the loop.

Syntax

while condition:

//do something

Example

>> looping_needed = True
>>
>>while looping_needed:
>># some operation on data
>>if condition:
>>   looping_needed = False

Print()

This function displays the output of a program. It is arguably more consistent when you're using the parenthesized version.

Example

```
>># this will work in all modern versions of Python
>>print("some text here")
"some text here"

>># but this only works in Python versions lower than 3.x
>>print"some text here too"
"some text here too"
```

Range()

A rang() function is the function that returns the list of integers to the sequence defined by arguments passed to it.

Syntax

argument variations:
range(terminal)
range(start, terminal)
range(start, terminal, step_size)

Example

>>range(4)
[0, 1, 2, 3]

>>range(2, 8)
[2, 3, 4, 5, 6, 7]

>>range(2, 13, 3)
[2, 5, 8, 11]

Sets

A collection of unique and unordered set of items. Some iterables can be converted into sets.

Example

```
>> new_set = {1, 2, 3, 4, 4, 4,'A', 'B', 'B', 'C'}
>> new_set
{'A', 1, 'C', 3, 4, 2, 'B'}

>> dup_list = [1,1,2,2,2,3,4,55,5,5,6,7,8,8]
>> set_from_list = set(dup_list)
>> set_from_list
{1, 2, 3, 4, 5, 6, 7, 8, 55}
```

Slice

This is a Python way of extracting "slices" or pieces of a list by using a special bracket notation which specifies the start and end of the section you wish to extract. By leaving the beginning value blank, it indicates that you wish to start at the beginning of the list. By leaving the ending value blank, it means you wish to go to the end of the list. If you use negative value references at the end of the list such as a list of four elements, -1 being the forth element. Slicing can be used as another way to yield yet another list, even if you just extract a single value.

Example

```
>># Specifying a beginning and end:
>>x = [1, 2, 3, 4]
>>x[2:3]
[3]
```

```
>># Specifying start at the beginning and end at the second
element
>>x[:2]
[1, 2]
```

```
>># Specifying start at the next to last element and go to the
end
>>x[-2:]
[3, 4]
```

```
>># Specifying start at the beginning and go to the next to last
element
>>x[:-1]
[1, 2, 3]
```

```
>># Specifying a step argument returns every n-th item
>>y = [1, 2, 3, 4, 5, 6, 7, 8]
>>y[::2]
[1, 3, 5, 7]

>># Return a reversed version of the list ( or string )
>>x[::-1]
[4, 3, 2, 1]

>># String reverse
>> my_string = "Aloha"
>> my_string[::-1]
"aholA"
```

Str()

Using this function will allow you to represent the content in which the variable is shown as a string. It provides the data type that the variable provides, but in a neat way. Str() cannot change the variable in place, instead it just returns it to the 'stringified' version of it. In more technical terms, str() calls a special _str_ method if an object is passed to it.

Syntax

str(object)

Example

```
>> # such features can be useful for concatenating strings
>> my_var = 123
>> my_var
123
>> str(my_var)
'123'

>> my_booking = "DB Airlines Flight " + str(my_var)
>> my_booking
'DB Airlines Flight 123'
```

Strings

These store characters using more built-in and convent methods. You can modify a strings content but they cannot be changed in place.

Example

```
>> my_string1 = "this is a valid string"
>> my_string2 = 'this is also a valid string'
>> my_string3 = 'this is' + ' ' + 'also' + ' ' + 'a string'
>> my_string3
"this is also a string"
```

Tuples

This is a data type that can hold an ordered collection of values but can be any type of values. The tuples are immutable which mean once they are created, they cannot be changed.

Example

```
>>x = (1, 2, 3, 4)
>>y = ('spam', 'eggs')

>> my_list = [1,2,3,4]
>> my_tuple = tuple(my_list)
>> my_tuple
(1, 2, 3, 4)
```

Tuple Assignment

These can be expanded into variables rather easily.

Example

```
name, age = ("Alice", 19)
# Now name has the value "Alice" and age has the value 19

# You can also omit the parentheses:
name, age = "Alice", 19
```

Variables

Variables are usually assigned to values by using the = operator. This is not to be confused with the == sign used for testing equality. A variable can hold any sort of value type such as dictionaries, functions and even lists.

Example

```
>>x = 12
>>x
12
```

www.ingramcontent.com/pod-product-compliance
Lightning Source LLC
Chambersburg PA
CBHW060939050326
40689CB00012B/2504